The Gate

AND OTHER POEMS ON A LIFE'S JOURNEY

POETRY BY DOUG JORDAN

PHOTOS BY SIDNEY SHAPIRA

FriesenPress

Suite 300 - 990 Fort St
Victoria, BC, V8V 3K2
Canada

www.friesenpress.com

ISBN
978-1-03-911051-9 (Hardcover)
978-1-03-911050-2 (Paperback)
978-1-03-911052-6 (eBook)

1. POETRY, SUBJECTS & THEMES, LOVE & EROTICA

Distributed to the trade by The Ingram Book Company

Table of Contents

Foreword   1

The Poet's Lament (1965)   6

The Golden Key (1968)   8

Reality (1968)   10

Imagination (1969)   12

The Leaf (1969)   14

Purple Butterfly (1969)   16

Sonnet 1 (2020)   18

Rhetoric of Revolution (1969)   20

The Speed of Dark (2020)   22

Lonesome Tree (1970)   24

Christmas Island (1983)   26

The Streets of Copenhagen (2011)   28

The Gate (2019)   30

Teacher (1971)   34

To My Student (1972)   36

There are many types of teachers These are but 4 of
them (2020)   38

The Funeral (1972)   40

The Chessman (1972)   **42**

A Walk In The Rain (394 Days) (2020)   **44**

After the Punishment to Fit the Deed (1973)   **46**

Ode to Plentiful Pollution OR How I spent my morning
Constitutional that day on Wellington Crescent in
1975   **48**

A Little Levity (1995)   **50**

The Search (1968)   **51**

To Todd (age six) A parent's lament (1982)   **52**

Star-Holder (1992)   **54**

Shilobrat (2020)   **56**

Research Blues (2019)   **58**

Wallflower (1993)   **62**

The Virus Wars (2020)   **64**

ô maître de tout (2020)   **66**

The Value of Respect (2020)   **68**

Latent Grief (2020)   **70**

The Leaves (2010)   **72**

The Flyer (2021)   **74**

Notes from the Poet   **77**

Acknowledgements   **79**

Foreword

I think it is 'poetic justice' that I have been putting off writing this foreword for several weeks, after having nudged 'the poet' sometimes to move forward, reflect, write something new, or rewrite something old. I understand the frustration that he might have felt, although it was never communicated.

In the fall of 2020, a new FB group led me to Mr. Doug Jordan, who had taught at Laidlaw School during my middle-school years, ending in June 1972. Doug had taken on 'all things drama', including extra-curricular clubs and concert evenings. This was my 'passion' at the time, and Doug had a way of making me feel special, encouraging me to write, act, and direct skits and plays for my grade and for younger grades. Doug's mentorship and support were among the several reasons I decided that I wanted to be a teacher.

Fast forward forty-eight years with no contact, and this was my chance to tell Doug how important he had been in my life. After a couple of FB Messenger exchanges, we met for coffee, and those forty-eight years just melted away. I learned about the loss of his dear wife in 2019. I heard all about his three children and four grandchildren, and learned that he is also living with Parkinson's Disease. I became aware that, in addition to twenty-six years as a teacher, Doug had also taken a law degree, and had practiced real-estate law for a few years before returning to teaching. Finally, there was his love of poetry and his blog, where he explores his life with Parkinson's, and tries out several different versions of poems, requesting feedback from his readers and often returning to the same poem over and over.

I was happy to tell Doug that he had made a real impact on my life. Drama remained a passion throughout my secondary years at St. Paul's High School. We talked about my thirty-three-year career as a teacher, consultant, and principal, in Transcona-Springfield and River East Transcona School Divisions. I shared how I had enjoyed teaching drama to my own elementary students, and that I had also presented workshops on 'drama in the classroom' through the Manitoba Drama Educators' Association.

About a week after our very enjoyable reunion, I received an email from Doug, asking if I would edit a book of his poetry. He also suggested that I could complement some poems with my photographs, a hobby that I have 'developed' since 2014. One caveat was that the photos should be in black and white, since his poetry tends to 'the dark.' *The Gate and Other Poems on a Life's Journey* is the collaborative result of this reunion of two retired educators, formerly teacher and student, now poet and photographer. Doug presented me with thirteen poems as the start of the book. As the weeks went on, he kept looking for a notebook full of old poems from the sixties. Doug began writing poetry as his teens turned to his twenties. He coyly admits one motivation was definitely "to impress the girls. And it worked." It took a month before Doug dropped off a very tattered legal-size manilla folder and a very worn duo-tang with poems scribbled on all four sides of its covers. Fast forward another couple of months, and Doug had amassed a collection of thirty-four poems.

As the title suggests, the writing of this book has been 'a journey.' I chose "The Gate" as the starting point and built the title around it. The reference to 'a gate with no fence' led me to show Doug some of my photos, in particular, the photo of an old gate in our Assiniboine Park. It now stands alone, a barrier to nothing. I always loved this photo, and it called out to me. "The Gate" was a poem Doug had first written and displayed on his blog, where at least three sequential versions can be found. The blog has been a sounding board for Doug, as his 'life's journey' took many twists and turns. It is a place where he speaks honestly about living with Parkinson's Disease, as well as about his grief over the loss of his beloved wife.

The collection grew and developed a life of its own. I read about the notion of the universal themes of poetry but decided to arrange the poems in chronological order, from Doug's late teens to early adult life, and I became comfortable with this approach to *A Life's Journey*. Nevertheless, I sensed that there were stops along the way that were missing. I asked Doug to write a poem about his late wife, ("A Walk in the Rain"), as well as a poem about his careers as teacher and lawyer ("The Value of Respect"). Then came my request for a poem about his life-long friendships made in his childhood, while living on the Shilo Army Base ("Shilobrat"). Ever the poet, Doug would write several drafts of each new poem, requesting feedback along the way. Our collaboration just worked, even with the restrictions of COVID-19 protocols. As the writing came to a close in January 2021, Doug sent me an email saying, "I think if it weren't for you, I would still be thinking I would like to write a book this summer." Indeed!

What do I bring to the process, in addition to my willingness to help move this project forward? Like the poet who expresses himself through words, and can elicit emotions from readers, I have found ways to do some of the same through my photos. With the exception of a few photos taken explicitly to illustrate a particular poem ("The Poet's Lament," "Rhetoric of Revolution," "The Chessman"), the majority of my photos were taken over the last seven years, using whatever cell-phone camera I owned. Most of the photos selected for the book were taken in Winnipeg, but others were taken in Ottawa, and as far away as Paris, France. My photos 'focus' on sky and clouds, architecture and art. They can be found on Google Maps, on my 365-day-a-year Facebook page, and in an online French-language magazine called, *le nénuphar*. It was a case of finding a photo to illustrate or complement a given poem, enhance the mood, or reflect the emotion. I transformed each photo into a black-and-white version of itself. I enjoyed the process of reading and rereading the poems, and spending hours scrolling through my photos in 'The Cloud.' I hope our readers will find the photos enhance the experience of reading Doug's poems, and do not distract. As the project unfolded, I sent Doug looking for a family photo to accompany certain poems that were written during or about his years as husband and father. Those photos are credited to the 'Jordan Family.'

Over the last six months, Doug and I have really gotten to know each other as adults and as friends. Recently, as we looked at the collection of poems in its final iteration, Doug sent an email in which he declared, "Isn't it strange, and somewhat comforting, that forty-eight years passed and we are not strangers."

Doug's poems never meet his own standards after one draft; for example, "The Streets of Copenhagen" took ten years to achieve 'finished' status. Doug adopted a fairly consistent style of writing rhyming poetry, which has sometimes caused him to wonder whether his poetry really had a place out in today's world. In order to gain some perspective, I consulted local author Harriet Zaidman who led us to the Winnipeg Public Library Poet-in-Residence, Lauren Carter. In no time at all, Ms. Carter read the poems and sent annotated feedback that Doug appreciated and used to improve his work. We would like to thank Harriet Zaidman and Lauren Carter for their gracious contributions.

At the very beginning of our collaboration, I asked Doug who his intended audience is for this book. He informed me, without hesitation, that it was being prepared with his family in mind, along with the group of friends referred to in "Shilobrat," and the many former students with whom he has developed close relationships. I count myself within those numbers. And so, with that legacy in mind, I am pleased to invite you to join us for *The Gate and Other Poems on a Life's Journey.*

Sidney Shapira
Photographer and Editor,
January 2021

The Poet's Lament (1965)

Reduced to using the other side
And writing even less
While watching television
And eating a frozen mess
When all upon a tuneful tale
I realize my fate
Unless I act most speedily
My poetry won't rate
I'll never make the *T.V. Times*
And *Maclean's* will close its door
While I sputter on and on
Writing even more
But then perhaps it's for the best
I must admit defeat
I'll leave this world a loser
Who didn't miss a beat

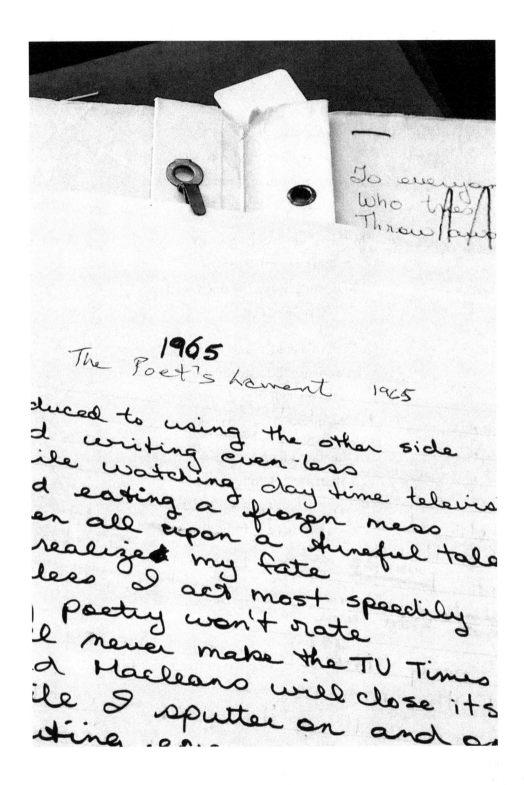

The Golden Key (1968)

A crowd of imbeciles
were dancing in a row
when a bearded man came upon them
with a golden key in tow

"My boys," he said in plaintive voice
"this key will open gates
and truth lies in the open yard
it only sits and waits.

"Take this golden key, my friends
and search for truth alone
for then you'll find the answers
to the questions you have known"

But the men sat and cringed in fright
then all took to their heels,
for fear of truth and what it holds
is common to imbeciles.

Reality (1968)

Reality will always be
Exactly what it seems
Expectations mostly turn
In life to broken dreams
So gather all your forces
And leave your thoughts behind
For man is what he's done and does
Not what he hopes to find

Imagination (1969)

Let me say sincerely
I don't know who I am
I plan to suffer greatly
Right up until the end
For my imagination
Controls with tyranny
My intrinsic mess
Ad ludicrum
And I never will be free

The Leaf (1969)

One day while walking in the park
A talking leaf I spied
A leaf that called to all the rest
In a pleading voice, it cried

"There's so much more to life you know
Than hanging around all day
Go someplace and find yourself"
But he heard a chorus say

"Of all the foolish things you ask
You really make us sad
To think of doing something else
You know, my boy, you're mad"

Winter came and snowy blasts
Sent life in search of covers
And that leaf died and fell to earth
Just like all the others.

Purple Butterfly (1969)

I chased a purple butterfly
And quickly fell behind
When suddenly it turned on me
And flew into my mind

It bored into my rebel brain
Then in the matter there
It laid a hundred thousand eggs
And hatched each one with care

A hundred thousand tiny troops
Worked both day and night
With mighty strength they wrenched my thoughts
And hid them from my sight

In formation as they toiled
Within my muddled brain
Correcting and completing thoughts
Till I knew I was insane

I gripped my hair and pulled it out
And rolled upon the ground
But still they searched each tiny thought
To correct the faults they found

Then one sullen summer day
The butterflies stood still
My head was filled with wondrous thoughts
But quite against my will

My life I lead is quiet now
It sets a quiet pace
It never veers to right nor left
it keeps me in one place
I would tell you more but there is naught to tell
My world's so commonplace

I am just another member of the stagnant human race.

Sonnet 1 (2020)

If I should live a million miles away
I would use my yearning mind to pick apart
The stars and rays I will not let stay
I will clear the path, right through my heart
As straight as cupid's arrows fly in flight
As righteous as the massive glow
It leads me to the blinding light,
The light that all the lovers know
It seems to me a journey fraught with risk
Intangibles negate the time
And temper it with an asterisk
Till you agree that you'll be mine

    And if my route was made in vain
    Then I hope we will meet again.

Rhetoric of Revolution (1969)

Rhetoric of revolution
Fought in smoky bars
Peace signs deftly painted on
1950 cars
Beards, beads, and crucifixes
Your challenge to the night
Empty salutations
For when the time is right

You say your mission's holy
And the means beget the end
So you call the people "brother"
And your enemy your friend
You ostracize your critics
Speaking words that they've all heard
From would-be Ché Guevaras
You're on the edge of the absurd

You spread around "the answers"
That you claim are to be found
In your endless fairy tales
And cacophony of sound
You put it all in chronicles
That never will be read
For before you find the answer
You'll have talked the question dead.

The Speed of Dark (2020)

While traveling at the speed of dark
I came upon a listener
I spoke to her of love and things
but just above a whisper
for fear that she would waste my time
and all my words would miss her

You see, you start with nothing
and the years go fading past
you win a few you lose a few
but you try to make life last
tho' in a bold Shakespearian way
some roles can be miscast

I had met her as a teenager
when her beauty was traditional
in fact, if one could summarize
her beauty was exceptional
I enjoyed her thoughts
but by the bye
her thoughts were existential

I lived up to her conditions
or at least I thought I tried
she said I was acceptable
but I knew at times she lied
we became inseparable
an ersatz king and bride

but I was a BMOC*
while she became sought after
her beauty and her brains were such
my reality was disaster
she went one way and I another
each trying to get there faster

Then nature intervened, we knew
our future was now forecast
I'd caught her on the straight away
but we both had finished last
so, I took my leave at the speed of light
no questions being asked
but in a quaint sub-rosa way
I shone behind my masque.

*BMOC - Big Man on Campus

Lonesome Tree (1970)

Lonesome Tree destroyed by fire
your bark begins to grow
and sunshine lights the hollow where
your darkened bowels show
the black within reflects my days
if fire cleans the slate
then Lonesome Tree move over please
before it's far too late.

Christmas Island (1983)

On Christmas Island south of Java
where the snow has yet to fall
sits a lady post-depression
painting pine trees on a wall

From within her shredded past
she pulls an ancient memory
of spruce and pine and bleeding hearts
a forest of her misery

With every stroke the past arrives
to sanctify the painted clime
gradually the wall fills up
with bent fir trees and frozen rime

She feels the wind bring biting snow
across the star-crossed ocean
she smiles at her self-rendition
and gets lost in pure emotion

She wonders if the whole is real
she fears her memories grow old
"At least," she says, "the winter's home."
but now she starts to feel the cold

She paints herself beneath the snow
a Christmas compromise
on Christmas Island, south of Java
an aged, white-haired painter dies.

The Streets of Copenhagen (2011)

On the streets of Copenhagen
supine, and bathed in red
I found a woman bleeding
from the thorns around her head

I stroked her hair, then gently
placed two coins upon her eyes
a genuflect to try to catch
the screams between her sighs

If only this were real
she whimpered in her sleep
Perhaps we might have had a life
And lived beyond the street

If only we were lovers
but I knew her soul was dead
and I was growing kind of weary
of the nails in our bed

I stooped to say the right things
but it came as no surprise
she was just an empty savior
full of saccharine and lies

She wiped her eyes with steel wool
her arms stretched out to keep
the shadow that could never mend
the wounds upon our feet

Lust became confusion
and demanded to be free
I told her I forgave her
and she did the same for me

In the streets of Copenhagen
where love is found for rent
it doesn't really matter
how your dignity is spent.

The Gate (2019)

There's a gate with no fence
but it's shut tight and locked
so stand on the outside and wait
my time is a thread
pursuing the lock
so I rest with my lust on the gate

And off in the mist
glowing hot lava
a woman of beauty and grace
her silks flow around her
ethereal seduction
I doubt she'll remember my face

We had spent time together
disguised as young lovers
that drive each other insane
but we did have our moments
neither surrendered
just anger without any pain

She comes too close beside me
she speaks to me sharply
then I'm hither and thither and yon
Make this night last forever,
and don't be discouraged
if you find in the morning I'm gone

But where would you go
I asked her at midnight
a time when we askers can't wait
I will just be a moment
she said through her smile
But I have to lock that old gate

I wanted to say
you are liquid today
your clothes seem to flow with the rhyme
I was eager to stay
and wash both your feet
and hopefully watch you wash mine

Perhaps I was anxious
perhaps I was frightened
perhaps there was no reason to stay
our button-down romance
had gradually faded
just gradually faded away

She came back in the twilight
should we start over
she had her heart on her face
I was righteously scolded
and relentlessly molded
and properly put in my place

Doug Jordan

You think I don't know you
You think you can have me
Well I won't suffer the disgrace
When we broke into pieces
You plied me with poems
But it was time you had to embrace

Her voice became softer
her sighs became stronger
she was certain her decision was right
she threw open the curtains
that remained in between us
and basked in the newly found light

In the mist we're a couple
I fidget she trembles
she's sweating while reading a line
you can lay here beside me
but first is an issue
before I will let you be mine

You must write me a poem
about no gate with a fence
and without any circular rhyme
that is my desire
my lust will recover
you just have to give me more time

This time I did give her
some red-carpet time
time that made much more sense
so here is that poem
so deliciously written
about love and an ungated fence.

Teacher (1971)

A teacher is a wise man
an idiot, a saint
depending on the time of day
your age and your complaint

He seems to ride you mercilessly
and never gives you rest
and offers the excuse that he
wants you to do your very best

He isn't such an ogre
and you really owe him much
but I'll tell you all a secret
and hope I have your trust

A teacher is a person
who when the day is through
knows you've given him so much more
than he ever gave to you.

Doug Jordan

To My Student (1972)

You sit intent with a book in your hand
and dream of creatures who
inhabit fairy tales of youth
and none can share with you
your dreams and wild imaginings
I once believed were true

It's hard to find that ducks can't talk
and Superman can't fly
that Bambi's just a story which
at one time made you cry
but everyone survives, although,
you'll sometimes wonder why.

The future is my gift, and yet,
may you be so bold
to have at hand your fantasies
to keep from growing old
for youth is such a fleeting thing
or so I have been told.

There are many types of teachers
These are but 4 of them (2020)

1

irritate

dominate

alienate

primate

a list of all the things you hate

2

fascinate

combobulate

alienate

apostate

this guy you should defenestrate

3

celebrate

complicate

arbitrate

surrogate

Not so bad not so great

4

illuminate

passionate

considerate

advocate

A list of all the things that rate

The Funeral (1972)

We laid him barefoot in his grave
and lowered him with care
sunglass hid the mourners' eyes
at least those who were there
a coffin costing six months' rent
we put into the ground
with thoughts of dripping taps at home
and all the time we'd found

The corpse looked up with open eyes
and saw the preacher's face
the tape-recorder lips that moved
his gowns of silk and lace
the people staring in the hole
the sun upon his head
the mounds of dirt that soon would fall
when all the words were said

The mourners turned to leave the yard
the corpse could only wait
for diggers to replace the dirt
before it got too late
his mind was filled (respectfully)
with thoughts of fellow man
he turned to be more comfortable
he didn't give a damn.

.

The Chessman (1972)

The chessman made a steady move
then crept into his mind
a way that would have won the game
how could he be so blind
"Good sir, a favour if you will
may I retrace my queen"
"You've made your move
play on, my friend
you can't go where you've been."

A Walk In The Rain (394 Days) (2020)

The very first day
With me and you in your space
near the hospital
where you studied
so certain a woman
you slowly but surely
imparted some certainty to me
You turned off the radio
and laid your book on the ground
You whispered a promising sound
Let's go for a walk
But it's raining I said
Makes it more interesting
came the reply
as you stripped
off your clothing
and concealed your virtue
with a coat made for rain
So would I
Are you going to join me?
Of course
And hand-in-hand
no remorse
our secret stayed secret
and we walked and talked
making some plans

including our wedding banns
I will never forget the wet streaks
I kissed off your cheeks
Sweet lady
Sweet memory of mine.

After the Punishment to Fit the Deed (1973)

I was a boy
tho' it may seem
if there ever was youth
it was all in a dream
but I looked at clouds
and saw dragons and things
and gryphons and wonderful
monsters with wings
and I fought in wars
that never came true
and performed fiendish deeds
on grasshoppers too

Yes, I was a boy
not too different than you
but at times I forget
what little boys do.

Ode to Plentiful Pollution OR How I spent my morning Constitutional that day on Wellington Crescent in 1975

O' yellow spot of snow upon
the snowy linen land
from whence you came, perhaps a dog
perhaps a fellow man
to mar the landscape, soft as down
beneath my willow feet
he left his mark, no doubt, no doubt!
pray God we never meet

For I as one who canst ignore
the beauty of my place
would take my fist and fast upon
would decorate his face
all lawmen should rise and take the sword
and strike the guilty hands
of those poor souls who canst control
the workings of their glands.

A Little Levity (1995)

A man has a dog that's a stray
It moves in a peculiar way
The dog has no legs
But still the dog begs
To go for a drag every day

The Search (1968)

I tried
they said
to end my search
to finish it somewhere
I looked awhile without result
yet it waits for me out there

I cried
they said
what's not can't be
I stopped for someone's sake
a grave of dreams sleeps alone
never more to wake

I died
they said
we will bury him
just where he'd want to be
I lie a thousand unwalked miles
between my dreams and me.

To Todd (age six) A parent's lament (1982)

Only the dogs are awake
And you
They from excitement
You from your fears
Which I will cure tomorrow
Wednesday at the latest.

Star-Holder (1992)

Lately I've been looking through new windows
and I've seen the future looking back at me
I am happy with the way you got life started
but still there are some things I'd like to see

I would like to see you searching for that moment
and reaching for the stars you hope to hold
forget about what everyone has told you
everything that glitters can be gold

And all those moments can turn into lifetimes
and all that glitter can glow even golder
if only you will look through my new windows
then grab the future firmly, my star-holder.

Shilobrat (2020)

This isn't that fair
my mind is quite bare
that's a problem because I can't write
I'm a poet who is writeless
and also quite sightless
the result is I'm feeling contrite

I avoid the condition
that leads to contrition
the backwash from talent's regime
and on that very note
there is something I wrote
so I turn to an earlier theme

It's nothing ersatz
they are called "Shilobrats"
I can call each member by name
I can ask for assistance
and meet no resistance
and offer them much of the same

Each one has potential
for becoming essential
in time and place that remain
It's a sweet dream of mine
that I'll wake up and find
I get to see them again

Now that was no chore
I could have written some more
but I'd have to begin with begat
There is much I could say
but let's leave it this way
I am proud to be called "Shilobrat."

Research Blues (2019)

I'm in the laboratory
Research is necessary
Livin' in a test tube
He's in the hallway
Looking for the payday
Man in a white coat
Pen out, pent up
Says he knows the reason
Coffee is in season

Get this. No joke
He's determined coffee
May help my "Parky D"

Test one we call count by seven
Adverse, perverse
Must do it in reverse
From 100
Remainder two

Got that still bad
It made my right hand start to shake
Then like some vicious magistrate
You have Parkinson's and that's great
You will make the perfect subject, mate

Get sick, think well
Take the meds without delay
Take four, four times a day

Maybe this is normal
It seems slightly formal
Perhaps a little carnal

The man says it's not time
Placebo, nocebo
We're trying to find his baseline
It's got to be yes or no
A secret that he doesn't know
Looking for another way
Anticipates the judgment day

He keeps hinting
It's something I did
No placebo nocebo
I be flippin' my lid

Kicking up the beach sand
Shaking in the right hand
A wobble when you do stand
Bruising when you meet land
He reminds me to follow fast
But I'm cruising in the quicksand

Doug Jordan

Noses supposes
No longer smell the roses
My thoughts safe in escrow
Living is a road show
I have to put my leg up
Shattering the man's cup
Call your secret commissary
Tell them it's not necessary
Giving you a promissory

First pill to last pill
Try to hold your body still
I waffle through a landfill
Chairman wants the minutes read
I recite my poems instead

In spite of all the brainfall
It's not another windfall
I try to hit a home run
But he's tossing me a spitball

Straight talk, bent walk
White coat docks the clock
Prod me when I'm symptom-free
Take a shot of coffee
I'm a million miles away
I feel like I want to pray
Vile liquid, kid
I have been coffee free for eternity

Look at me
I took a chance
Rolled up the lid
Congrats to me for all I did

Don't guess at remedies
Night, night, sleep tight
We are all nearly right
Don't let the spasms bite
Now the day is in the can
Datum found and data ran
Let me know the things you see

Using a confession booth
He's telling me his empty truth
He thinks it's level two PD
Don't believe so
It's shouting level one to me

At least it can't be three
I am not enamoured by PD

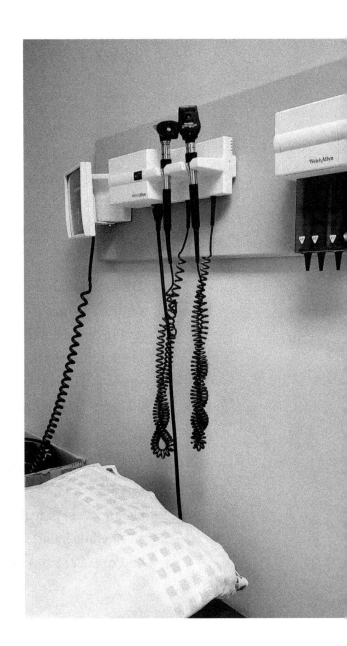

Wallflower (1993)

The queen of the shades
lurks in the shadows
lost in her mind and her moods
her yearning torments her
the music is soaring
she stands in her corner and broods

Her thoughts are a maze
of one-way turns
and in one she wallows and sighs
she can't understand
the call of the wild
a howling that creeps from her thighs

She enters the circle
and sways to the centre
but nobody knows she is there
she picks at her nails
so carefully painted
and runs her hand through her hair

Then if by some magic
her hand is rerouted
he takes her hand by surprise
they move to the music
delaying the darkness
that covers her heart and her eyes

Just for a moment
she encounters enjoyment
her happiness comes and it fades
she won't let them see
the queen with a smile
she rules the land of the shades.

Doug Jordan

The Virus Wars (2020)

Most survived the first phase
we averaged five a day
but then the bastard hit us
in a new ingenuous way
it danced among the old and frail
in its darkest kill foray

Our allies to the south of us
where we all had placed our bets
held the world's greatest armory
but let us not forget
you can't destroy a virus
with a fancy sabre-jet

So the generals turned to science
while the deaths kept piling high
they were working on an answer
but they could not verify
an adequate solution
so the world was on stand-by

And every living citizen
was asked to wear a mask
and keep their distance socially
a pretty easy task
but half the population
refused the ungodly masque

The US civil war arose
in twenty-twenty-one
but there was no clear decision
as to which side God was on
that didn't stop Great Leader
claim his side had clearly won

It seemed he was their patron
rule by one man
he got rid of all detractors
to fight on without a plan
he looked across the border
like some deluded super fan

"We need to take your water
and I mean every drop
we will divert your rivers
resistance will not stop
my glorious well-armed forces
will ensure you lose the lot"

We smiled at his arrogance
he thought that we would flee
we will defend the border
all the world will see
we made a pledge to Canada
to stand on guard for thee
and so we stand here waiting
it is twenty twenty-three.

ô maître de tout (2020)

I relinquish
all doubt
that religion's a farce
why worship a god
made of glue
you stuck to a plan
ignoring my prayers
that apparently were
foreign to you.
you took from my life
the one certitude
our plans could really come true.
Et maintenant je me demande
comment aimez-vous
mon amour qui est morte?
Je ne sais pas
ce qu'elle pensera de vous.
Adieu,
ô maître de tout.

The Value of Respect (2020)

Each house is an island
anonymous living
each with a different take
from atop of Lil's hill
I see junkyards and mansions
rewards for the choices some make.

High five for the teacher
who lives in my brain and cannot
afford an estate
(just to be thorough a
pleasant down-low for those
in a house with a gate).

I do not revile
the men with a gate
they probably deserve their success
I was there too
I had the degree
but in fact
I could not have cared less.

They offer me wages
and money to spare
high society all in one glance
I study the future
to make my decision
I'm not ready to make it by chance.

I have no objection
to the lords of the manors
for once it was part of my plan
if not for an itch
I might've been rich
but I scratched and found a straw man.

Something inside me
kept calling me back
loud like a preacher
lawyer to teacher
I moved from mansion to shack.

What irony now
I am richer than Coresus
no money as you suspect
an abundance of friendship
my scholars bequeathed me
my fortune—a bountiful bond of
respect.

Latent Grief (2020)

If memories no longer make me cry
and misery ... cold misery
no longer occupies my gutted mind
my search for life in days gone by
will still start and stop with you.

Your scented smiles and ever
touching grace
our life ... brief life
grows colder and finds me memory
blind.
Still, I have the need to find a place
to spend more time with you.

At night, in dreams, I know some
relief
and sleep ... warm sleep
wakes up the cold darkness
unrefined
and sunlight displaces all my grief
I walk hand-in-hand with you.

The Leaves (2010)

The Leaves
exit the trees
like bewildered bats

rising
   and
      falling

on a whim
to settle at last
on the dying grass

But I ...
I look to their empty roosts
and see
only summer.

The Flyer (2021)

I will teach her to fly, he said to himself, while watching the bounce in
her stride
he remembered his past, uncertain, unsure
until something inside him had died.

And nobody noticed, for nobody cared
they missed the fact he had wings; so shaken with doubt,
he turned to himself to quietly do other things.

But now was his chance, to recover his passion
and break his long bond with the earth. She will fly in her moment
and soar in his future and prove to the others his worth.

He'd never achieved flight, for lack of a mentor, and his chains
anchored deep in the ground. No complainer was he,
a fourth-place contender, where losers are usually found.

In the back of his thoughts, he started to mumble
with an echo in the halls of his mind; she must defy gravity
for that is the measure by which we would leave loss behind.

She was nervous that day, but somebody noticed
and I quietly belayed all her tears. It was her turn to discover
the rapture of flying while confidently facing our fears.

She trotted up lightly and with controlled fury
she launched without any strain. He had taught her to fly
and that magic of flight had rattled the links of his chain.

After all of the years, he could relax and enjoy her
his work being finally done. She could fly with best
and he smiled at the clincher......
the loser had finally won.

Notes from the Poet

I don't have structure when I create. I just go walking, and the rhymes are walking with me. Most of the time, I struggle to keep on task, but even then, my bohemian way will worm itself into my world, and I will be left trying to find a rhyme with "garden" or "orange."

I enjoy poetry that rhymes and has rhythm. It is easier to read. Most poets prefer a form of free verse and their message is completely lost to many of their readers as they try to uncomplicate the poet's words. This is when, as a teacher, we often hear "I hate poetry." No wonder. They can't understand it, and don't get me going on Shakespeare and others of that ilk.

I say, if you are a poet and have a message or a story to tell, try do so in its most understandable terms. So, I present my poetry and some thoughts behind the writing.

Purple Butterfly - While attending Brandon University, I was torn between campus radicalism and the values that my parents had instilled in me.

Being twenty-two years old, I was naturally drawn to campus politics, and I wrote for the campus newspaper, and in addition, I wrote some poems that I now consider to be rather trite; however, they are reflective of what I now term "academic pablum" or the education beyond the walls of the halls of academia, represented by the purple butterfly—an elusive little bugger!

I wanted to be a true rebel, but I was pablum-free upon graduation.

Christmas Island - I was reading a map, and I noticed the phrase "Christmas Island South of Java" that somebody had written in the margin, and I loved the music in that phrase and the poem wrote itself.

A Walk in the Rain - This was written 394 days after my wife's death in September 2019, and I miss her terribly. Latent grief came much later and is described in the third-to-last poem in this collection.

The Funeral - Not much to say; those are the words that erupted from my brain while watching a funeral procession.

The Gate - I was running down a rural road when I saw an old gate, but there was no fence surrounding the yard, just a gate, and I couldn't let it pass. My brain was stuck on the smooth symmetry: "a gate with no fence."

Research Blues - This poem details my role in a medical-research project in which the scientists looked at the question, "Does caffeine have any effect on the progression of Parkinson's Disease?"

The Value of Respect - I was standing atop "Lil's Hill," the highest ground in Winnipeg. It's named after former city councillor Lillian Hallonquist, whose committee was given the task of turning an old city dump into a recreation area, now officially known as "Westview Park." People always ask me, "Why would you become a teacher when you could be a lawyer?" My response is "I never had fun as a lawyer, but I had fun every day as a teacher." My decision resulted in many good friends. Don't get me wrong, I found the study of law to be interesting, but the practice was fairly mundane.

Latent Grief - As I write this, it has now been 484 days since my wife passed away, and I am afraid her countenance is fading, but I still remember all of her when she visits me in my dreams, and I can feel she is alive. Check out this third-to-last poem.

Doug Jordan
March, 2021
Winnipeg, Manitoba

Acknowledgements

Doug and Sid would like to thank the following people for their support, and for their specific contributions to the completion of this project.

The FriesenPress Team in Victoria, B.C.

Don ("Fabulous George") Jordan

Denise Belanger

Jack M. Shapira

Lauren Carter

Harriet Zaidman

Judy and Tyler Morgan

Photo Credits

All photos in this book are the work of Sidney Shapira, with the exception of the photos accompanying the following poems:

Teacher, p. 35, by Kylie Golding

A Walk In The Rain, p. 45, courtesy of the Jordan Family

To Todd, Age 6, p. 53, courtesy of the Jordan Family

Shilobrat, p. 57, courtesy of the Jordan family

Author Photo by Doug Jordan

Photographer Photo by Denise Belanger

CPSIA information can be obtained
at www.ICGtesting.com
Printed in the USA
LVHW062205221021
701183LV00005B/530